NEBRASKA

Jill Foran

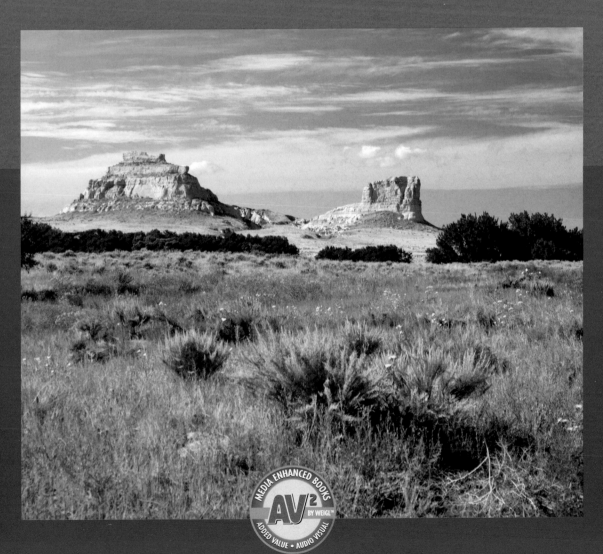

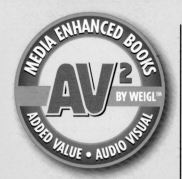

AV² provides enriched content that supplements and complements this book. Weigl's AV² books strive to create inspired learning and engage young minds in a total learning experience.

Your AV² Media Enhanced books come alive with...

Audio
Listen to sections of the book read aloud.

Key Words
Study vocabulary, and complete a matching word activity.

Video
Watch informative video clips.

Quizzes
Test your knowledge.

Embedded Weblinks
Gain additional information for research.

Slide Show
View images and captions, and prepare a presentation.

Try This!
Complete activities and hands-on experiments.

... and much, much more!

Go to **www.av2books.com**, and enter this book's unique code.

BOOK CODE

D 9 4 6 5 8 6

AV² by Weigl brings you media enhanced books that support active learning.

Published by AV² by Weigl
350 5th Avenue, 59th Floor
New York, NY 10118
Website: www.av2books.com

Names: Foran, Jill, author.
Title: Nebraska : the cornhusker state / Jill Foran.
Description: New York, NY : AV2 by Weigl, 2016. | Series: Discover America | Includes index.
Identifiers: LCCN 2015048023 (print) | LCCN 2015049098 (ebook) | ISBN 9781489648969 (hard cover : alk. paper) | ISBN 9781489648976 (soft cover : alk. paper) | ISBN 9781489648983 (Multi-User eBook)
Subjects: LCSH: Nebraska--Juvenile literature.
Classification: LCC F666.3 .F677 2016 (print) | LCC F666.3 (ebook) | DDC 978.2--dc23
LC record available at http://lccn.loc.gov/2015048023

Printed in the United States of America, in Brainerd, Minnesota
1 2 3 4 5 6 7 8 9 20 19 18 17 16

082016
210716

Project Coordinator Heather Kissock
Art Director Terry Paulhus

Photo Credits
Every reasonable effort has been made to trace ownership and to obtain permission to reprint copyright material. The publisher would be pleased to have any errors or omissions brought to their attention so that they may be corrected in subsequent printings. The publisher acknowledges Getty Images and Alamy as its primary image suppliers for this title.

NEBRASKA

Contents

STATE FLAG
Nebraska

STATE BIRD
Western Meadowlark

STATE ANIMAL
White-tailed Deer

STATE FLOWER
Goldenrod

STATE TREE
Cottonwood

STATE SEAL
Nebraska

Nickname
The Cornhusker State

Motto
Equality Before the Law

Song
"Beautiful Nebraska," words
by Jim Fras and Guy G. Miller,
music by Jim Fras

Population
(2010 Census) 1,826,341
Ranked 38th state

Entered the Union
March 1, 1867, as the 37th state

Capital
Lincoln

Discover Nebraska

Nebraska is a state of treeless prairies, fertile croplands, and grassy, rolling plains. It lies halfway between the Atlantic and Pacific Oceans. The Platte River flows across the state, offering its waters for **irrigation**, recreation, and the production of **hydroelectric** power. The river is also indirectly responsible for the state's name. The Oto, who were among the first Native Americans to live in the area, named the Platte River *Nebrathka*, which means "flat water."

Nebraska is nicknamed the Cornhusker State after its main agricultural crop. Corn harvesting and the removal of husks were once done by hand. Large cornfields, wheat fields, and vast grazing lands have earned Nebraska the reputation as one of the world's best agricultural regions.

Although the state is known for rolling farm land, it actually has a diverse terrain featuring sandhills, forests, bluffs, and prairies. The panhandle of Nebraska is in the northwestern region of the state and offers stunning buttes and a rugged landscape. Omaha and Lincoln are Nebraska's two biggest cities and have bustling economies combined with museums, sports, and a cowboy cultural heritage.

The Land

The Homestead National Monument of America, in Homestead, Nebraska, commemorates the pioneers who traveled west to settle the land.

The first nickname for Nebraska was **"The Tree Planter's State,"** because of the millions of trees planted by Nebraska settlers.

At almost **23,000 miles**, Nebraska has more miles of **river** than any other state.

Covered wagons were the most common form of transportation through the Great Plains in the mid-1800s.

Beginnings

In the mid-1800s, thousands of pioneers crossed through Nebraska. The Platte River Valley became a westward route as people from the East headed for the rich farmland of Oregon and the gold mines of California. The Oregon, California, and Mormon Trails were all very important routes that followed the Platte River as well as other river valleys.

At this time, Nebraska was regarded as little more than an access route to the West. Pioneers traveled through the region, mistakenly assuming that the dry land would be difficult to farm. The region was flat, sandy, and treeless. These features prompted the Nebraska region to be labeled the Great American Desert. As time passed, settlers decided to farm Nebraska's "desert," and they began to discover the rich resources the land had to offer.

Today, most of the land in Nebraska is used for farming and grazing. Thanks to large irrigation systems, land that was once believed to be too dry for agriculture now yields an abundance of crops. Good soil for farmland has become one of Nebraska's most valuable resources. Also, the state's Sand Hills and grasslands are now vast grazing ranges that support large herds of cattle. Nebraska's agricultural abundance is not just a source of food. It is also a source of pride for many of the state's residents.

Where is
NEBRASKA?

Nebraska is bordered by six other states. South Dakota is to the north of Nebraska, while Iowa and Missouri are to the east. Kansas lies to the south. Colorado is to the west and south, and Wyoming is to the west. The Missouri River forms Nebraska's entire eastern border and part of its northern border.

United States Map

Nebraska

Alaska Hawai'i

MAP LEGEND

■ Nebraska

☆ Capital City

● Major City

▲ Ashfall Fossil Beds State Historical Park

■ Indian Cave State Park

☐ Bordering States

☐ Water

1 Lincoln

With a population of more than 270,000, Lincoln is the second-largest city in the state. It was founded in 1854 and chosen as the state capital in 1867. Lincoln is a regional center of government, finance, commerce, arts, education, and health care.

2 Ashfall Fossil Beds State Historical Park

The Ashfall Fossil Beds feature prehistoric animals preserved at a watering hole. It is believed they died there after a massive volcanic eruption about 12 million years ago. Guests can visit the park to watch the ongoing excavation of native American rhinos and ancestral horses.

SOUTH DAKOTA

Missouri River

IOWA

NEBRASKA

2

1

☆
Lincoln

Omaha ○

4

3

KANSAS

N

SCALE

0   50 miles

3 Indian Cave State Park

Bordering the Missouri River, Indian Cave State Park features 3,052 acres of rugged terrain. The park offers remote camping and 22 miles of hiking trails. History lovers can experience the restored schoolhouse at St. Deroin, an abandoned river town from the 1850s.

4 Omaha

The largest city in Nebraska was founded in 1854. Today, Omaha has a bustling waterfront and downtown district, and is the home to Fortune 500 companies and the Union Pacific Railroad. It also features the Bob Kerrey Pedestrian Bridge, a 3,000-foot-long walkway across the Missouri River.

Land Features

Nebraska's landscape consists of fertile, rolling plains. These plains are divided into two major land areas. The Dissected Till Plains cover the eastern fifth of the state. Several thousand years ago, glaciers covered the area. As the glaciers melted, they left behind debris, which served as the basis for extremely fertile soil. Today, the area is made up of lowlands dissected, or divided up, by rivers and streams.

Most of Nebraska's landscape is dominated by the Great Plains, a land area that is largely grassland. The Sand Hills of the north-central part of the state are an interesting feature of the Great Plains. These vast hills were formed by the wind blowing sand that was originally deposited by glaciers. Today, grasses help keep the sand in place.

Toadstool Geologic Park

Toadstool Geologic Park is located in the Oglala National Grassland in western Nebraska. It gets its name from the unusual rock formations in the park that look like toadstools. Fossils of prehistoric animals have been found in the park.

Platte River

The Platte River flows southeast across Nebraska before emptying into the Missouri River. Pioneers followed the river west on the Oregon, California, and Mormon Trails. More than a dozen dams on the river have decreased its width.

Great Plains

The Great Plains run north–south through the continental United States. They stretch from Montana to Texas, including much of Nebraska. They are a vast, high region of semiarid grassland.

Sand Hills

The sloping hills and valleys of Nebraska's Sand Hills cover about one-fourth of the state. They are located in the north-central and northwestern part of Nebraska.

Climate

Nebraska experiences great seasonal changes in its weather. Winters can be bitterly cold, and summers can be uncomfortably hot. The weather can also change quickly.

Warm air from the Gulf of Mexico occasionally collides with cool air from the north, which can result in severe weather. In 2014, Nebraska had more reports of large hail than any other state. Tornadoes, blizzards, and violent thunderstorms are all common in the state.

Nebraska's weather is unique. It is not uncommon to see great extremes in temperature throughout the year. The lowest recorded temperature in Nebraska was –47° Fahrenheit at Oshkosh on December 22, 1989. The highest recorded temperature was 118°F at Minden on July 24, 1936.

Average Annual Precipitation Across Nebraska

There can be great variation in precipitation between west and east Nebraska. Why might the eastern part of the state receive more precipitation than the west?

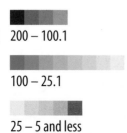

LEGEND

Average Annual Precipitation (in inches) 1961–1990

200 – 100.1

100 – 25.1

25 – 5 and less

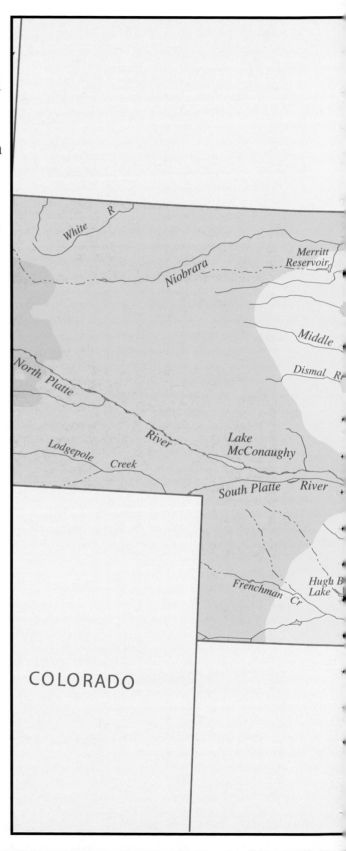

COLORADO

MINNESOTA

SOUTH DAKOTA

Merritt
servoir,

River

Lewis and Clark
Lake

Middle

North

Goose

Cr

Missouri

Logan Creek

Dredge

IOWA

Dismal River

Loup

Elkhorn

Loup

Cedar River

Shell Creek

River

South Loup

R

R

R

Loup

River

River

Big

Wood

River

Platte

Medicine Cr

Hugh Butler
Lake

River

Blue

N Fk

Big

MO

Nemaha R

River

Harlan
County
Lake

Little

Blue

River

Beaver Cr

Republican

R

R

KANSAS

N

Scale 0 ▬▬▬ 40 Miles

The Loup River is a tributary of the Platte River. The Loup River is 68 miles long and helps to irrigate agricultural areas on the eastern edge of the state.

Nature's Resources

Water is one of Nebraska's greatest natural resources. The Ogallala aquifer is a reserve of water located deep below most of Nebraska. Parts of this aquifer extend through Kansas, northwestern Oklahoma, and northwestern Texas.

Water from the aquifer is pumped to the surface, and some of it is used to irrigate agricultural land in the region. Water is also stored in some of Nebraska's soil. In the Sand Hills, the soil acts like a sponge, absorbing and holding the area's rainfall. There are also more than 80 lakes in the state, as well as the Missouri River and all of its tributaries.

Nebraska's rich soil comes from deep deposits of **loess** in the eastern, central, and south-central parts of the state. Loess helps form some of the best agricultural soils in the country. More than 95 percent of Nebraska's land is used for agricultural purposes such as farming and ranching.

Fertile soil and water are not the only natural resources Nebraska offers. Among Nebraska's important minerals are limestone, sand, and gravel. Petroleum is found in the counties of Cheyenne, Hitchcock, Kimball, and Red Willow.

In 2014, more than 3 million barrels of crude oil were produced in Nebraska.

Each spring, 10.3 million acres of corn are planted in Nebraska.

Vegetation

As only 2 percent of its land is forested, Nebraska is not well known for its trees. It is, however, known for its tree planting. In 1872, Nebraska became the first state to celebrate Arbor Day. A leader named J. Sterling Morton convinced the state board of agriculture to set aside a day to plant trees on the state's almost treeless landscape. In 1885, Arbor Day became a legal holiday in Nebraska, and today it is celebrated in many states throughout the country.

A large portion of Nebraska's hand-planted trees can be found in the Nebraska National Forest. The forest was established in 1902 as an experiment to see if trees could grow in the Sand Hills region. With about 22,000 acres of the forest planted by hand, it is the largest human-made forest in the United States.

Bluestem Grass

Bluestem grass is native to Nebraska's prairies. There are several varieties, including little bluestem and big bluestem. It is often used as an ornamental grass in landscaping.

Goldenrod

Goldenrod has bright yellow flowers and can grow up to 4 feet high. It blooms in late summer and early autumn. Some people use the leaves for teas and medicinal purposes.

Cottonwood Trees

Cottonwood trees can be either male or female. The female trees produce fluffy white seeds that give the tree its name. Cottonwood trees often grow beside rivers.

Wild Bergamot

Wild bergamot is a member of the mint family. Its flowers are red, pink, white, or lavender. Plants can grow as high as 5 feet. The leaves can be used to flavor tea.

Wildlife

Millions of years ago, prehistoric animals roamed the Nebraska area. Scientists have uncovered fossil remains in Sioux County in the northwest corner of the state. Fossils of mammoths and **mastodons** have been found there. Other fossils from Sioux County suggest that Nebraska was once a tropical land. **Paleontologists** have uncovered remains of saber-toothed tigers, crocodiles, and rhinoceroses.

In more recent times, huge herds of bison, or buffalo, roamed Nebraska. Today, Nebraska's wildlife consists mostly of small animals such as the badger, coyote, fox, muskrat, jackrabbit, raccoon, skunk, and squirrel. Mule deer also roam much of the region, and antelope and elk are found in the northwest. Game birds such as pheasants, quail, prairie chickens, and wild turkeys are all plentiful on Nebraska's prairies. The state's waters are full of bass, carp, trout, pike, crappies, and perch.

Prairie Dog

The black-tailed prairie dog is the only prairie dog species found in Nebraska, in the western two-thirds of the state. Prairie dogs are highly social animals. Their colonies can be recognized by the holes and mounds at the entrance. A colony has as many as 50 burrow entrances per acre.

Prairie Rattlesnake

The prairie rattlesnake lives in the grasses of western Nebraska's Great Plains. In the winter, the snakes live together in sites that do not freeze, such as the burrows of other animals. They feed on small mammals.

Prairie Chicken

The prairie chicken is a game bird of the grouse family. Adults grow up to 18 inches long. During courtship, the male inflates air sacs in its throat. It makes booming noises from these inflated air sacs.

Pronghorn

Pronghorns can be found only on North America's Great Plains. The male's horns average about 12 inches and are shed yearly. The female sometimes develops smaller horns. With a top speed of 60 miles per hour, a pronghorn can outrun any animal that chases it.

Economy

Carhenge

Carhenge, near Alliance, is a re-creation of ancient Stonehenge in Wiltshire, England, but in place of giant stones, the builders of Carhenge used old cars. In 2009, Carhenge was named the second wackiest attraction in the United States.

Tourism

Nebraska has many natural, historical, and cultural attractions. Tourists may retrace the water route of the Lewis and Clark Expedition, view fossil excavation sites, or visit the Strategic Air and Space Museum near Eugene T. Mahoney State Park. Visitors can experience the beauty of Nebraska even while passing through the state. Nebraska's Highway 2, which runs through the center of the state, has been categorized as a scenic byway.

Nebraska is a great place for history buffs. Several forts and pioneer museums offer a glimpse of what life was like for Nebraska's early settlers. The Stuhr Museum of the Prairie Pioneer allows visitors to relive Nebraska's past with Old West **memorabilia** and Native American artifacts. There is also a railroad town in the museum that takes visitors back in time, with 60 original buildings from the late 1800s.

Henry Doorly Zoo

Omaha's Henry Doorly Zoo is ranked one of the best zoos in the nation. It has a huge aquarium and the world's largest enclosed rainforest. Hubbard Gorilla Valley is a $14 million, three-acre exhibit at the zoo.

Scotts Bluff National Monument

Scotts Bluff towers 800 feet above the North Platte River. It was a landmark for thousands of settlers who crossed the Great Plains in covered wagons in the 1800s. At Scotts Bluff National Monument, summertime visitors can relive life on the Oregon Trail through a living history program.

Chimney Rock National Historic Site

Chimney Rock is one of the most famous landmarks on the Oregon, California, and Mormon Trails. The rock formation rises nearly 300 feet above the surrounding North Platte River valley. Its peak is 4,226 feet above sea level. It is estimated that nearly half a million settlers saw Chimney Rock as they made their way westward.

There are more than 23,000 corn farms in Nebraska.

Primary Industries

Agriculture is a vital part of Nebraska's economy. Nebraska ranks third, behind Texas and Kansas, for its number of beef cattle. Hog production is also important to Nebraska's economy. The Cornhusker State is a leading corn producer. Its annual corn crop is the third-largest of any state in the country. Other important crops in Nebraska include soybeans, hay, sorghum, and wheat.

Nebraska's agricultural goods are central to food processing, one of the state's other major industries. The food manufacturing industry uses the state's agricultural products as its **raw materials**. Nebraska is one of the nation's chief producers of meat and grain products. Large meatpacking plants can be found in Dakota City, Fremont, Grand Island, Lexington, Omaha, and Gibbon. Breakfast cereal, livestock feed, and bread are all important grain-based products processed in the state.

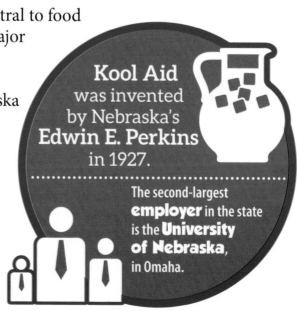

Kool Aid was invented by Nebraska's **Edwin E. Perkins** in 1927.

The second-largest **employer** in the state is the **University of Nebraska**, in Omaha.

Value of Goods and Services (in Millions of Dollars)

Although Nebraska is known as an agricultural state, many different industries are important. Which other industries could be thought of as offshoots of the part of the economy that is directly agricultural?

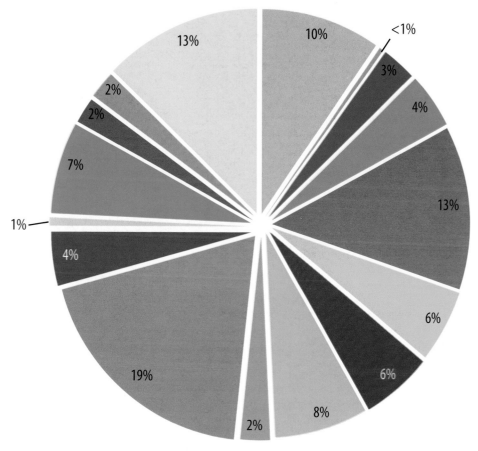

Agriculture, Forestry, and Fishing $10,199

Mining..$351*

Utilities...$3,022

Construction...$4,663

Manufacturing $13,730

Wholesale Trade $6,099

Retail Trade ....$ 6,135

Transportation and Warehousing $7,994

Media and Entertainment $2,587

Finance, Insurance, and Real Estate...........$20,292

Professional and Technical Services $4,530

Education $745

Health Care..$7,699

Hotels and Restaurants................................$2,162

Other Services $2,313

Government $13,552

*Less than 1%

Both Union Pacific and BNSF Railway have major rail lines through Nebraska. Easy access to rail lines assists Nebraska's agricultural and mining industries by making it easy to ship goods to various markets.

Goods and Services

Nebraska's central location is responsible for its thriving transportation industry. For hundreds of years, people have used the Platte River Valley as a transportation route. In 1865, Omaha became the eastern **terminus** of the first transcontinental railroad in the United States. Railroad companies then began laying track westward, making Omaha an important center for railroad transport. Today, the Union Pacific Railroad has its headquarters in Omaha, and other major rail lines also provide freight service to the state.

Many Nebraskans have jobs with the federal or state government. Government services in the state include the operation of electrical utilities, public hospitals, and military bases. The headquarters of the United States Strategic Command, or USSTRATCOM, are on Offutt Air Force Base near Omaha. The Command Center controls the country's bombers and long-range missiles.

The U.S. Strategic Command is located at Offutt Air Force Base near Omaha, Nebraska. It is one of nine defense centers in the U.S.

With a large number of teachers working in the state's schools, the public school system is a major employer in Nebraska. Students are given many opportunities for higher learning in the state. The University of Nebraska, which opened in 1869, has campuses in Omaha, Lincoln, and Kearney.

More than 25,000 people are enrolled at the University of Nebraska, in Lincoln.

For the majority of the year, the Pawnee lived in large, dome-shaped lodges.

Hunting bison was crucial to the Native American groups that lived in Nebraska and the surrounding plains states. Bison meat and hide were important to groups in the area, such as the Cheyenne, for both economic and cultural reasons.

Native Americans

Centuries before European explorers made their way to Nebraska, many groups of Native Americans lived in the area. Among those who farmed and hunted along the rivers were the Mission, Omaha, Oto, and Ponca. The Pawnee were the largest group to settle along Nebraska's Platte, Republican, and Loup Rivers. They hunted bison and grew crops such as corn and beans.

The Pawnee believed that some of the stars were gods. They used their knowledge of the stars to regulate activities such as planting corn. They also thought of corn as a symbolic mother through whom the Sun god gave blessings to the people.

Native American groups in western Nebraska, including the Sioux, Comanche, Cheyenne, and Arapaho, relied mostly on hunting for their livelihood. These groups were all **nomadic**, meaning they lived in temporary villages. Their livelihood depended on hunting, so these groups followed the bison herds and often worked together to protect their hunting grounds from the Pawnee and early European settlers.

Religion was a major focus in the life of the Sioux people. The most important religious occasion was the yearly Sun Dance. At this ceremony, groups of Sioux gathered to perform acts of individual and community sacrifice, which they believed would maintain their connection to the universe as a whole.

Exploring the Land

In 1541, the Spanish explorer Francisco Vázquez de Coronado led an expedition across the southwestern United States. Coronado claimed a large area for Spain that included present-day Nebraska. In 1682, René-Robert Cavelier, sieur de La Salle, traveled down the Mississippi River. He claimed all the land drained by the Mississippi River for France. La Salle named this vast area Louisiana after his king, Louis XIV. By the end of the 1600s, both Spain and France had claimed the Nebraska region without any Spanish or French citizens setting food in the area.

Timeline of Settlement

U.S. Exploration

1803 The United States purchases the Louisiana Territory, including Nebraska, from France.

1804 Lewis and Clark's expedition to explore the Louisiana Territory passes through Nebraska.

1714 Étienne Veniard de Bourgmont establishes a trading post on the Platte River.

1806 Zebulon Pike explores southern Nebraska.

1682 René-Robert Cavelier, sieur de La Salle, claims Nebraska for France.

1810 A fur trading post is established at Bellevue.

Early Exploration

Étienne Veniard de Bourgmont, a French explorer, is the first European on record to have entered Nebraska. In 1714, he traveled up the Missouri River to the mouth of the Platte and built a trading post. In the early 1800s, what is now Nebraska was part of France's Louisiana Territory. In 1803, the United States bought this vast tract of land in the western Mississippi River basin. Soon after, President Thomas Jefferson sent Meriwether Lewis and William Clark to explore the territory.

1848 Fort Kearny is built to protect settlers on the Oregon Trail.

1854 Nebraska is made a separate territory by the Kansas-Nebraska Act.

1843 Pioneers begin traveling in large numbers through Nebraska on the Oregon Trail.

1861 The **Pony Express** passes through Nebraska, carrying mail from Missouri to California.

1820 Fort Atkinson is established by the U.S. Army.

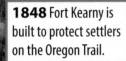

1867 Nebraska becomes the 37th state.

U.S. Territory and Statehood

Many settlers traveling the Oregon Trail crossed the Platte River while making their way through Nebraska.

The First Settlers

Explorers and fur traders from the eastern United States followed Lewis and Clark to the Nebraska wilderness. In the early 1800s, several trading posts were built along the Missouri River. To protect its newly claimed territory, the U.S. government built Fort Atkinson in 1820. It was home to as many as 1,000 people, mostly soldiers and their families, until it was abandoned seven years later.

In 1854, the U.S. government passed the Kansas-Nebraska Act. This act created the Kansas and Nebraska territories and opened the region for settlement. Settlers from the eastern states began to arrive. Nebraska's first towns sprang up along or near the Missouri River. By 1860, more than 28,000 people lived in the region.

The Homestead Act of 1862 brought a rush of eager pioneers to the Nebraska Territory. The act granted 160 free acres of western **frontier** land to any settler who farmed it. Settlers would own the land after they had farmed it for five years.

Farming was challenging for Nebraska settlers, as the tough roots of the prairie grasses made it difficult to work the soil.

During the late 1800s, the new farmers had plenty of bad luck. They suffered through some very cold winters and long periods of drought. There was also a brief period when swarms of grasshoppers plagued the area, ruining crops. Many farmers left the plains, but those who remained benefited from improved farming techniques, and over time, more and more settlers moved to Nebraska.

The early settlers of Nebraska often used sod, the top layer of soil and grass, to build homes. The sod was good insulation against the harsh Nebraska winters.

History Makers

Many notable Nebraskans have contributed to the development of their state and their country. One even became the president of the United States. Other people helped minority groups fight for their rights. Some Nebraskans wrote books and produced films about the U.S. experience. Businessmen and religious leaders have helped other people achieve success and made Nebraskans proud.

Willa Cather (1873–1947)

Willa Cather was a novelist noted for her portrayal of pioneer life on the plains. She grew up in Red Cloud and used her memories as material for her writing. Her best-known books about Nebraska are *O Pioneers!* and *My Ántonia*.

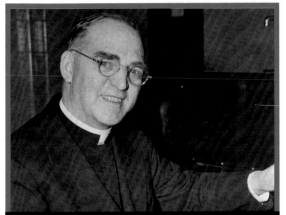

Father Edward Flanagan (1886–1948)

Father Edward Joseph Flanagan founded Father Flanagan's Home for Boys in Omaha in 1917. This was a home and school intended to provide support and education for neglected or troubled boys. The home was moved west of Omaha in 1918 and quickly became incorporated as Boys Town. Eighty-one similar programs around the world now operate based on Father Flanagan's example.

Gerald R. Ford (1913–2006)

Gerald Ford was born in Omaha but moved to Michigan as a child. He served in Congress as a representative from Michigan for 25 years. Then he served as vice president. In 1974, he became the United States' 39th president when Richard Nixon resigned.

Malcolm X (1925–1965)

Born Malcolm Little in Omaha, Malcolm X became a vocal leader in the early 1960s. He joined the Nation of Islam, also known as the Black Muslims, and helped increase the group's membership. He urged African Americans to take pride in their race. His writings, including *The Autobiography of Malcolm X*, continue to inspire many people.

Warren Buffett (1930–)

Warren Buffett grew up in Omaha. His father was a stockbroker and served as a U.S. congressman. At an early age, Buffett showed a knack for financial matters. He took control of the manufacturing company Berkshire Hathaway in 1965. Buffett has been slowly giving away large shares of his company, decreasing his total net worth. In 2015, he gave $2.8 billion, split between five different charities.

Culture

The median age range for residents of Omaha is 34.2, two years younger than the state's median age range.

For every square mile of Nebraska there is, on average, 24 people. Nebraska is ranked 43rd in the U.S. for population density.

The People Today

According to the 2010 U.S. Census, Nebraska has a population of about 1,826,241. Its population had grown by almost 7 percent in the decade from 2000 to 2010. In the early 1900s, more than two-thirds of Nebraskans lived in rural areas. As time passed, this number shifted dramatically. Many people left rural areas due to the growing employment opportunities in the state's towns and cities. Today, most Nebraskans live in urban areas.

Omaha is a bustling city with more than 430,000 residents. Lincoln, Nebraska, has about 270,000. Of Nebraska's population, 89 percent are Caucasian, and 10 percent are Hispanic or Latino.

Nebraska's population **increased** by more than **115,000** people from 2000 to 2010.

Q What are some of the reasons that many people from other states and other countries are choosing to move to Nebraska?

The Nebraska capitol building is constructed of Indiana limestone. Construction started on the building in 1922 and was finished in 1932.

State Government

Nebraska's government is unique among all the states in the nation. Like other states, Nebraska has an executive branch of government that is headed by a governor. Like most other states, Nebraska has a judicial system that is headed by a Supreme Court. However, Nebraska is the only state in the Union to have a **unicameral** legislature. Every other state legislature has two houses, or chambers, not one.

Nebraska's legislature was not always unicameral. In 1934, Nebraskans voted to rid themselves of half their state legislature. People felt that a unicameral formation would be more democratic and would allow more public awareness of the legislature's actions. In 1937, the first session of the state's unicameral legislature was held. Today, there are 49 members in the legislature. These members are referred to as senators, and each serves a term of four years.

The doors to the legislative chambers were designed to honor the Native Americans of the Great Plains.

Nebraska's state song is called
"Beautiful Nebraska."

Beautiful Nebraska, peaceful prairieland, Laced with many rivers,

and the hills of sand; Dark green valleys cradled in the earth,

Rain and sunshine bring abundant birth.

Beautiful Nebraska, as you look around,

You will find a rainbow reaching to the ground; All these wonders by the Master's hand;

Beautiful Nebraska land. We are so proud of this state where we live,

There is no place that has so much to give.

* excerpted

The ornamentation in the entrance of the state capitol is meant to represent the "Gifts of Nature," with the Sun at the center of the ceiling in a medallion.

Czech Days, in Nebraska, is a celebration of the Czech culture and community. Traditional dancing, food, and parades are held over a long weekend in August.

Celebrating Culture

During the 1800s, thousands of Europeans came to Nebraska in search of free or inexpensive land to farm. German, Swedish, Czech, and Irish **immigrants** flocked to the region. Many people who live in Nebraska today are their descendants. They work hard to preserve the cultural traditions of their ancestors.

A large number of the state's ethnic communities are concentrated in specific villages or towns. The village of Wausa, for example, has many people of Swedish descent. The Wausa Community Swedish Smorgasbord is held every October. For more than 50 years, the event has celebrated Swedish traditions with colorful costumes, food, and music. In Wilber, the annual National Czech Festival showcases Czech culture with arts, crafts, and food.

Nebraska's Native Americans actively preserve and share their cultural traditions through colorful and lively **powwow** celebrations. During the first full moon in August, the Omaha Tribe of Nebraska hosts a powwow to celebrate the harvest. This powwow is the oldest harvest celebration in the state.

There are many events and sites throughout Nebraska that pay tribute to the state's frontier and pioneer heritage. Cowboy museums in Gordon and Ogallala recognize the ranching traditions and activities that continue to be a large part of Nebraska life. Pioneer museums, festivals, and landmarks showcase Nebraska's important historic figures and events. Every year in Lincoln, Nebraskans celebrate their state during the Nebraska State Fair, which features Nebraskan talent, including local arts and crafts.

For nearly 150 years, more than 70 Native American groups have been participating in the annual Winnebago powwow in Nebraska.

In Ogallala, Nebraska, the pioneer store fronts have been maintained to honor the history of Old West settlements in the state.

Arts and Entertainment

Many popular entertainers are from the state of Nebraska. Actors such as Nick Nolte, Marlon Brando, and Henry Fonda were born in the Cornhusker State. Other well-known Cornhuskers include Fred Astaire, a dancer and film actor, and comedian Johnny Carson.

The state supports many impressive theatrical troupes and programs for theater, music, and dance lovers. Omaha is a major center for the arts in Nebraska. Among the city's theaters are the Omaha Theater Company and the Omaha Magic Theatre. The Omaha Community Playhouse is among the largest community theaters in the United States and boasts a professional touring company called the Nebraska Theatre Caravan.

Fred Astaire was born in Omaha, Nebraska. He was a stage, film, and television star for almost 76 years.

Students at **Bellevue University** can take a **college course** about radio personality **Rush Limbaugh**.

Omaha native **Nicholas Sparks**, who is best known as author of *The Notebook*, has sold more than **100 million** books worldwide.

The performing arts thrive in other parts of the state, too. The Lincoln Community Playhouse puts on engaging performances, and the Lincoln Symphony Orchestra entertains listeners with musical works. The Lied Center for Performing Arts, at the University of Nebraska at Lincoln, presents nationally and internationally recognized performers and speakers.

The Lied Center for the Performing Arts was built in 1990. Its mission is to "educate, inspire, and entertain the people of Nebraska" through theater.

Nebraska is as rich in visual arts as it is in performing arts. Omaha's Joslyn Art Museum has one of the finest art collections of the American West in the country. The Sheldon Memorial Art Gallery and Sculpture Garden is on the grounds of the University of Nebraska at Lincoln. It has fascinating displays of twentieth-century North American paintings and sculpture as well as eighteenth-century landscapes and still-life paintings.

The Joslyn Museum in Omaha works to preserve fine art and educate its visitors. The building itself is one of the best examples of Art Deco architecture in the U.S.

The University of Nebraska football team has had three Heisman trophy winners in its history. The Heisman Trophy is awarded to the best college football player of a particular season.

Sports and Recreation

There are no major professional sports teams located in Nebraska, but Nebraskans' commitment to college athletics is outstanding. The University of Nebraska recruits and trains some of the finest young athletes in the country. Cornhuskers teams compete against other colleges and universities in such sports as football, volleyball, basketball, and baseball.

The college football season draws Nebraska's most lively and enthusiastic fans. The Cornhuskers are traditionally a strong football team and have finished many seasons as one of the top teams in the country. They have also won numerous conference championships.

The University of Nebraska **Cornhuskers football team** has attended a **record-breaking 27** consecutive bowl games.

The University of Nebraska–Lincoln's weight lifting room is the **largest in the country,** at three-quarters of an acre.

Nebraska is known for its rodeos. The state's first rodeo was put on in the 1880s by William Cody, known as Buffalo Bill Cody. Buffalo Bill was one of the best-known cowboys of the Old West. In 1882, it is thought that Buffalo Bill organized the first official rodeo in the nation. Today, the Buffalo Bill Rodeo is held every June near the town of North Platte.

One of the state's most popular rodeos is called Nebraska's Big Rodeo and is held each July in Burwell. In fact, Burwell's rodeo grounds are active all summer long with ranch rodeos and professional rodeos. There are several other county and community rodeos held throughout the state.

The Buffalo Bill Rodeo is part of Nebraskaland Days. It was first held in 1882.

The Big Rodeo, held in Burwell, Nebraska, has been an annual tradition since 1921. It is just one of the many rodeos held throughout the state each year.

Get To Know
NEBRASKA

Lincoln is the site of the National Museum of Roller Skating. It has the world's largest collection of historic roller skates and roller-skating memorabilia.

There are approximately 49,000 farms in Nebraska.

Nebraska was the first state to complete the United States' interstate program, with Interstate 80. In 2007, I-80 celebrated its 50-year anniversary.

The Reuben sandwich was invented in Omaha, Nebraska.

The state insect is the honeybee.

The first **frozen dinner**, or TV dinner, in the world was packaged in Omaha in 1953.

In Waterloo, Nebraska, it is against the law for barbers to eat onions between 7 a.m. and 7 p.m.

Brain Teasers

What have you learned about Nebraska after reading this book? Test your knowledge by answering these questions. All of the information can be found in the text you just read. The answers are provided below for easy reference.

1 What is an unicameral legislature?

2 Malcolm X was born in which Nebraska city?

3 What did the Homestead Act of 1862 promise to early settlers?

4 In 1872, Nebraska became the first state to celebrate which holiday?

6 Which city is the largest in Nebraska?

5 What is Nebraska's greatest natural resource?

7 With the Louisiana Purchase, the United States bought a large amount of land, including Nebraska, from which country?

8 In which year did Lewis and Clark pass through Nebraska?

ANSWER KEY
1. A legislature with only one house. 2. Omaha 3. 160 free acres to anyone who farmed it for at least 5 years. 4. Arbor Day 5. Water 6. Omaha 7. France 8. 1804

Key Words

frontier: land that forms the furthest boundary of inhabited regions

hydroelectric: water-generated electricity

immigrants: people who move to a new country

irrigation: supplying dry land with water through human-made processes

loess: a yellowish sandy soil that is carried by wind

mastodons: large, extinct, elephant-like mammals

memorabilia: souvenirs and historical items associated with particular times or subjects

nomadic: moving from place to place, often in search of food

paleontologists: scientists who study prehistoric remains, such as fossils

Pony Express: a system of mail delivery in the mid-1800s. Mail carriers rode ponies between Missouri and California.

powwow: a Native American ceremony or festival

raw materials: materials that have not yet been processed but will be used to make a product

terminus: the end of a railroad route

unicameral: a legislature that consists of only one house

Index

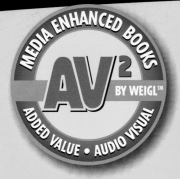

Log on to www.av2books.com

AV² by Weigl brings you media enhanced books that support active learning. Go to www.av2books.com, and enter the special code found on page 2 of this book. You will gain access to enriched and enhanced content that supplements and complements this book. Content includes video, audio, weblinks, quizzes, a slide show, and activities.

AV² Online Navigation

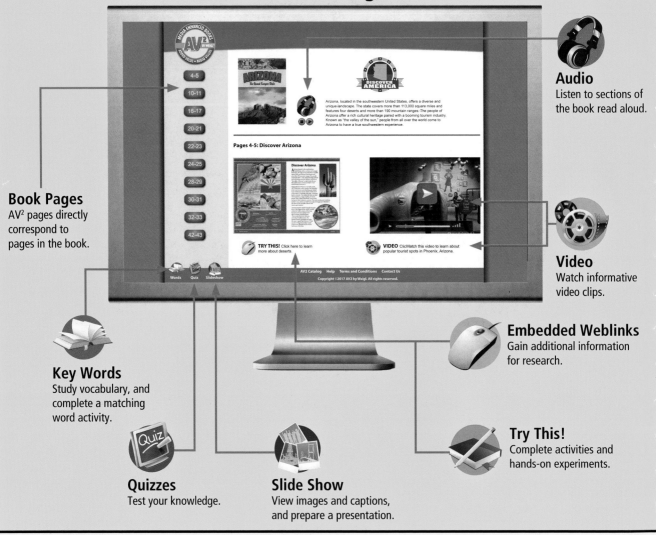

Audio
Listen to sections of the book read aloud.

Book Pages
AV² pages directly correspond to pages in the book.

Video
Watch informative video clips.

Embedded Weblinks
Gain additional information for research.

Key Words
Study vocabulary, and complete a matching word activity.

Try This!
Complete activities and hands-on experiments.

Quizzes
Test your knowledge.

Slide Show
View images and captions, and prepare a presentation.

AV² was built to bridge the gap between print and digital. We encourage you to tell us what you like and what you want to see in the future.

Sign up to be an AV² Ambassador at www.av2books.com/ambassador.

Due to the dynamic nature of the Internet, some of the URLs and activities provided as part of AV² by Weigl may have changed or ceased to exist. AV² by Weigl accepts no responsibility for any such changes. All media enhanced books are regularly monitored to update addresses and sites in a timely manner. Contact AV² by Weigl at 1-866-649-3445 or av2books@weigl.com with any questions, comments, or feedback.